First published in Great Britain 2025 by Jack Solev

This publi[cation ...] 2025.

Jack Soley has assert[ed ...] [t]he Author of this work in accordanc[e ...] [...] [P]atents Act 1988.

All rights reserved. No part of this publication may be reproduced, stored in a retrieval system, or transmitted in any form or by any means, electronic, mechanical, photocopying, recording or otherwise, without the prior permission of the publisher.

A catalogue record for this book is available from the British Library.

All opinions are of that of the author and do not represent the views of the publishing company or their affiliates.

This book is published by Pomerak Ventures Ltd, registered in England & Wales under the company number 15578139.

POMERAK
ventures

ISBN: 9781917706087

Contents

Introduction 6

Remember, you're a writer 9

Fresh Potatoes 11

Espresso Martini 13

Haiku for Sir Keir Starmer 14

Haiku for the weaklings 15

HN54 FTC 16

Little Impacts 18

Monopoly 20

The Jewellers 23

In Charge 24

Gare de Monaco 25

Birmingham Bins 26

What can we do when we dream? 27

Limerick to my hometown 29

Change of Heart 30

Wiltshire Pride 32

Stale Doughnut 33

Losing my keys 34

Trip to the Barbershop 36

More Martinis 37

I Smell Petrol	38
7:10 Dreamer	40
Midnighter	41
High Street Town Centre	42
All the Prime Ministers	44
Haiku for the bored	46
Podcasts	47
Kebabs in the shop	48
War is a Lie	49
Haiku for Selling a Car	50
Sunburn Sadness	51
No^{No} (The Power of No)	52
Amnesia	53
What's a Religion?	54
Haiku for the Painstricken	55
Inspirational Messages	56
Monologue on Wood	57
Metric World	59
Questions That I Can't Find Answers To	60
Tesco Generation	61
Hard to Understand	62
Proverbs To End	63
Outroduction	64

Acknowledgements 68

Introduction

Wow, can you believe it's been about 3 years, 6 months, and 15 days since I took my first steps into the amazing world of writing? That was the day I officially became an author! I've had the pleasure of publishing books on fun topics like 2 on Sandboarding, 1 about changing names, an art book, a translation of that art book, and even 3 fun facts about obscure facts! I'm a very non-fictional man as you could possibly tell, as I think fiction as a writer is difficult to get into and from a reader who would be used to my style of writing, I could only suspect that it would be more than hard to adjust.

I've always had a bit of a soft spot for poetry, starting way back when I first heard W.H. Auden's Night Mail in school. As a Year 10 student, it seemed totally natural to me to try to turn it into a rap and put a beat behind my reading of the poem.

I should explain that such an event never took place and a Night Mail rap never was, but I was fascinated my the meter of poetry, how much information could be condensed into this passage, or any passage; the fact not all poetry has to rhyme, haikus, the shortest poems are less than a few letters long, sonnets, seriousness, satire, and all the toys that go with poetic reading, and I figured that poetry could be anything you want it to be.

My main motivation for this poetry book was that I come up with poems and mantras in my daily life and being the natural writer I am (presumably), I want to document them and because of Max Fosh. Yeah, that guy who's the kind of prankster who doesn't cause any genuine harm to anyone, he wouldn't dare hurt a fly even if he's got a fly swatter in his hand ready to swat; haven't met him but genuinely an inspiration who's I feel we share ideas of a similar calibre, like catching a fish from the Thames and cooking it for himself to make fish and chips, the only difference is, he has the balls to follow through with his ideas. But yeah, back to Fosh; he wrote a poetry book consisting of his friend's messages, I wouldn't say it's of a standardised poetic style but who am I to judge? It became a number 1 bestseller, of course it did! It's Max Fosh, he'll probably manage to convince the Prime Minister to press the red button on the Trident nuclear submarine!

Anyway, enough about Max and back to the stacks of writings that I've come up with and wanted to share with the world, will this be a poetry book bestseller? Probably not. Will I fulfil an aspiration by making a collaboration of inspirational and affirmational poems and prose and releasing into a book for the population to indulge? Absolutely. I shall share them with you.

Remember, you're a writer

Yes, I'm a writer
A visual exciter
Informative reciter
Creative spark igniter

Let's fire up the brain
The neurons are my flame
The words flow like blood
Language becomes a flood
My books on the bookshelf, filled to the brim
But haiku's, poems, they're too trim

Thoughts on paper, the prose moves mountains
Ideas and creation, flow swift like fountains
Fiction, comics, stories never fail
But facts above all, shall forever prevail

Never ever has context let me down
But ambiguous text? That makes me frown
I'd rather read instructions, timetables, a tale of stardom
Than sit alone on the shores of boredom

So remember this, and it cannot be flawed
The pen is mightier than the sword
My writing passion shall refuse to be stopped
I will never fall prey to writer's block

So yes, I'm a writer remember my name
You can forget old drafts, they bought nothing but shame
You can't ruin my inspiration, there's too much time I spend
And you can guess this poem's coming to its end.

But this poem, this mantra, the affirmation of which I speak
Is it unique? sleek? amateur? or tongue-in-cheek?
My words, letters, linguistic tricks do they impress, or go straight through?

Well, I'll leave it to you.

Fresh Potatoes

I thought I'd plant a potato
Just to see how much it can grow
Large bags full of soil in the garden
Lack of water with the culprit a hot sun
Twas the advent of growing a potato

Days passed and no foliage had sprout
Patience waned and plants I wanted to throw out
Plenty of water fed to my edible babies
Expecting growth certainly had me at ease
Not enough to flood, nowhere close to drought

The green plant had grown from the earth
Under the soil, the shoot amassed its girth
Some of the fruits of my labours taste sweet
Other vegetables in salads go down a treat
But this fine potato, would be rich in its worth

Dig deep and rip away at this hard-working soil
Take these potatoes, bring them to the boil
Many recipes of which you can get to grips
If you're feeling lazy, homemade chunky chips
But be careful, not to drown them in too much oil

These spuds like natural foods are nutritious
When dug up, I bet the farmers are wondrous
Whether it's a pie, jackets, or mash
These tubers don't cost a lot of cash
Eat those potatoes, they're simply delicious.

Haiku for Sir Keir Starmer

Anger for farmers
Labour victory with ease
We raised council tax.

Espresso Martini

An espresso martini a day, fades all your troubles away

Make that number double, you're on a staircase to trouble

Will you make it triple? My god, you sure love to tipple

Wait, you had four? No wonder you're on the floor

Did you consume five? How are you still alive?

After six you're mad, actually no, it's getting a bit sad

Seven down, you're not stopping? We need to prevent the 8th helping

But after eight, it's too late, and there's nothing more to say; you'll feel the hangover come the very next day.

Haiku for the weaklings

Don't fear of your build
Lack of strength is a blessing
No heavy lifting.

HN54 FTC

HN54 FTC
That's my car you see!

It's a black Citroen C3 hatchback,
Practical, economical, and room for a roof rack.

Survivor of tough road trips to the airport,
A frequenter to the continent via the seaport.

The car has been so generous to me,
Getting me from A to B, without a huge fee.

It coped with a nail deep in the tyre,
This was during a weekend I spent in Hampshire.

I'm saving this jalopy for another fine experience,
No doubt I'll press the engine hard much to its inconvenience.

If you find my motor on the wide open road,
Look out for bumper stickers as there's one with a toad!

There's also flags of the nations which I've toured,
No expense spared, with the amount of fuel poured.

Yes, my wagon's a fair diesel couldn't you tell?
I used to use vegetable oil when I couldn't afford Shell.

The veggie oil was truly hard to start during a cold spell,
That hatchback chugging along had a pure, fatty smell.

I've called this banger a spaceship it's truly an odd shape, It's still holding out on the road it's simply no jape.

HN54 FTC is the steed that belongs to me,
The happiness it's given me I also it grants to thee.

Little Impacts

An elder woman ventured onto my bus, her shades were red and this is what she said: "that drive was beautiful, you should be a chauffeur".

That comment made my day, I respected her, the world smiled at me so I smiled right back, many shifts prior: smiling was an action I lack.

The job was a drain, turning up was a pain. Somehow, I'm still here but having the guts to look for other work, it's something that gives me fear.

Another woman said I was slow, she missed her appointment and it was a big blow, everyone was late, not just you! The negative mood that day didn't fade, it simply grew.

These comments fuelled sadness in my work, discouraging words gave me the impression that in this trade, there was no perk.

I can't fault driving in this job, it's the roads that give me trouble; too fast and I'll wreck the bus, too slow it'll be quicker walking on the rubble.

Fast forward 2 months after writing this, life's going well and I'm living like it; I lost my excitement and the love for the work had gone, one day I had enough, I quit.

Advance another 2 months I'm in a job I love, I program car keys, cut them, among other things too; I've never stopped smiling in my new job, even when I'm cobbling a shoe.

Monopoly

I want to play a game! A game you say? A game I say! Let's play Monopoly, a fast-paced game dealing property.

I'll choose the Top Hat, looks fancy, and I like to go the whole hog, but the main reason is that someone else chose the dog.

I first roll a 9, everything seems fine, Pentonville Road. I'll buy it! I'll build my light blues I'll grab the whole set, still got enough cash to live the life of a London jet set!

My strategy it seems is to play the game with ease, I'll claim everything I land on, like the British Empire in the year 1751.

Opponents roll dice and I watch over, they're buying the properties and reigning over, pity me if I land on their deeds, rent I must pay and they'll have too much money for their needs.

Gameplay marches on, by sheer luck I end up on Park Lane, you know if I buy this, to everyone else's dismay, I can build up an empire and be a right pain!

I rolled a 7, landed on chance, I hope this card serves me well... Oh bother, I'm making a trip to a jail cell. During hard time, I watched with envy as my rivals rolled with skill, until race car rolls an 8, He bought Mayfair, that stopped my brief thrill.

I pondered to have a deal, negotiate, it's only fair because there's many other properties I could build a collection, build houses here and there.

You know, it'll be silly for me to pay so much for property. I'll sell it to you with glee, for an exorbitant fee, and it's my knowledge that you won't bankrupt me, you can't afford to put houses on the blues, tee hee!

Race car accepts my offer, I know he can't build on his blues, he's already been hammered by a community chest card to pay his hospital dues.

Some time later, the Iron looks as he's playing with all the luck in his hand, good saving, lucky throws, he completed the reds after buying the sought after Strand.

Nothing I can see is out of place, I rolled a 3 and hopped onto the free parking space; we're playing the normal rules, we're doing things by the book, if we were playing custom rules, all that tax money I'd have happily took!

The dog is looking timid, they own all the rail stations, and a small pair of browns, even with hotels, low expectations!

Race car gets money again, has enough to buy houses, actually make it 5. If you land on what was a cheap Mayfair, you'd be lucky to see it alive.

I survived it, with cash to spare, passed Go to collect my £200, picking up my money like it was in stacks, then I realised passing Go is a time machine to paying Income Tax, what an anticlimax.

Nobody's landing on the properties by the Iron, those reds and purples don't look a decent investment, and no wonga to expand or build a development.

Alas, it was my birthday, so a tenner from the race car, iron, and dog came my way. I still couldn't grab the last light blue, nobody landed on it but I'd plenty of money to pay.

Rolling continues, chaos ensues, many a properties and there's no time to share, new houses and hotels, here and there. I have one set, my streets are orange.

Threw a double 2, can I take a chance? I'll take that chance, I'm feeling optimistic, opponents have many a mortgage, seems like there's a cash shortage. Sure I'll survive a shock, no matter the block but I be aghast! Advance to Trafalgar Square, owned by Iron with their many houses, time to mortgage my oranges and rid those green houses on them, that didn't last!

Everyone else is raking in their wealth, my situation is simply poor health, I'll be out the door, penniless and poor, another double could lead me to survive, not snake eyes though! Double one, that's the end of my enterprise.

I'm on the Park Lane I used to own, now I'm the victim of a £1,500 rent on that race car's large red home. Is this a joke?! I'm a debtor to all as of recent and as a result, I'm completely broke.

Call this a bankruptcy, my ending to this game is upon me and that's that. But could it have been all because I chose that fancy Top Hat?

The Jewellers

I like looking at watches in jewellers,
it helps me pass the time.

In Charge

Can I lead this team?
Can I? Can I?
I can prove I'm worthy enough
I can! I can!

Please give me this chance to take command
Please! Please!
I will be straight-talking and won't let you down
Believe me! Believe!

Did you want me to take control?
I want to! I really do!
The tasks will be done and the trash will be gone
It will! It will!

Now I'm leading, I'm the boss, and I run this crew!
I must ask, "what can I do for you?"

Gare de Monaco

Across from the coffee shop
Sits a bookshelf and a plug socket
I'll donate the book I finished reading
Walk in the toilet, close the door and lock it.

You thought I'd say pocket?
What a fool you are!
But I shouldn't be too cocky,
I've been waiting 3 hours for my train.

Should have taken the car.

Birmingham Bins

Birmingham bins aren't being collected
Refuse collectors ain't ever respected
Six-figure salaries for figures elected
Blue collar workers pay offers rejected.

Border force on strike in ports across the nation
Can't fly to Málaga, I'll have to have a staycation
Might visit Eastbourne, Lyme Regis, or Dover
It'll be nice to pay my gas bill when this is all over.

I'll get seen by my doctor if I break my knee
15 hour wait time? That's what you get for free!
I could go private, star service, same day
Does your clinic take Klarna? I can't afford to pay.

Back to the bins, they're overflowing their load
Mice playing footie with an apple core in the road
All cause Birmingham bins still ain't collected
Fly-tipping is the norm, you can't get arrested.

Army's called to assist, instead of boots on foreign soil
All because the council lay deep in their pool of turmoil
Will this tragedy end? Or is this just the mere beginning?
The bins have been collected, but where's it all going?

What can we do when we dream?

It's amazing what we can do when we dream:

We can fly over a corn field
Marry our lovers
Become fighters
Re-live memories that be permanently inscribed
Feel alive in a world when we'd otherwise be frail
Accomplish achievements, never fail
It's amazing what we can do when we dream.

It's amazing who we can be when we dream:

We can be the hero that everyone's wanting to be
Or the villain that stops order, maximising chaos
The Lagos businessman wishing to make it big
A Queen, with a court jester: "give me a jig!"
The fastest driver in the land
A football star looking for those trophies in my hand
It's amazing who we can be when we dream.

It's amazing where we can live when we dream:

That silent, secluded ranch where you hear pins fall
Huge mansion, swimming pool, with tennis courts
The old fort looking out to sea
In the big city, just a room big enough for the dog and me
Atop the roof like the villain I am
Lighthouse keeper? I can watch cars caught in a jam
It's amazing where we can live when we dream.

It's amazing what powers we have when we dream:

Nobody can ever tell us 'no'
I can fly high, I can fly low
Become invisible, the phantasm you crave
Read my mind? Or change it shall you be brave
I'd have a power where I'd double everything I touch
Like an inventory, I could also consume your lunch!
It's amazing what powers we have when we dream.

Limerick to my hometown

Swindon's the town on a hill that's high
Slowly becoming the place where dreams come to die
Initially an innovative place, it fell from grace
Everything's closing, the town centre's a disgrace
That town of Swindon that's on a hill that's high.

Change of Heart

I am the greatest, not modest
Kill your debtors, spare no-one
Born with respect, nothing need be earned
Hopes shall forever be ignored, chase hate
Money is more important than education
Love gluttony, hate helping others
I do what I want, you can do your thing later
Do crime, no point getting out there to shine
What's the point in life, I get a kick out of suffering
You are not above me, we'll never be equals.
Ignore your parents, listen to your false friends
Drugs are a safe haven, sobriety is a living nightmare
The necessary need is revenge, forgiveness is petty
Carrying that weapon can save you, religion locks you up
Shrug off wisdom, take in spontaneous advice
Be a fool, never pander to hand of friendship
Embrace danger it's a saviour unlike safety
Rudeness defines your attitude, what's respect?

Wait.. Wait.. What am I doing? Where am I going wrong?

Respect defines your attitude, what's rudeness?
Embrace safety it's a saviour unlike danger
Pander to the hand of friendship, never be a fool
Take in wisdom, shrug off the spontaneous advice
Carrying that weapon locks you up, religion can save you
The neccesary need is forgiveness, revenge is petty
Drugs are a living nightmare, sobriety is a safe haven
Listen to your parents, ignore your false friends
I'm not above you, we'll always be equals
What's the point in suffering, I get a kick out of life
Shine, no point in getting out there to do crime
I do what you want, I can do my thing later
Love helping others, hate gluttony
Education is more important than money
Hate shall forever be ignored, chase hopes
Born with nothing, respect need be earned
Kill no-one, spare your debtors
I am modest, not the greatest.

Wiltshire Pride

Every time I see the flag I raise my hand, I salute
The white horses on the hill, the views, such beaut
English evergreen plains, quiet villages, the peace
Army barracks, firing ranges, trucks housing military police.

That one major restaurant chain, one town, Swindon
A country manor with its grandeur, no animals, Wilton
Anglo-Saxon ruler lie here, over one of many Avons, Malmesbury
Stone circle nearby, consecrated cathedral, Salisbury.

There are six counties that Wiltshire touch, landlocked much
Canals and rivers running up, down, side to side, like the Dutch
That old bird back on the scene on the plains, a Great Bustard
Stirring up more local pride, green hills, daisies, wild mustard.

Driving out of my home, I feel pain, I betray my roots
Coming back to see the beautiful shire, I eagerly walk in my boots
Heavenly cuisine awaits: a Wiltshire cure, Devizes pie, lardy cake
My county calls me home, forever loyal, every minute I stay awake.

Stale Doughnut

O oily cake, why must you be hard and challenging to chew?
Even after leaving you for 4 days, what else did I do to you?
You're hard to the touch, my teeth attempt to clamp this treat
Looking divine when I bought you, now downgraded to the street.

O greasy confection, why when I bite you risk me infection?
Back in the days of education, having you in class, risk detention
The glaze on your body be glistening, shining from yards across
Consume too many of you, rotten teeth, sugar overdose, floss.

O sweet treat, why must you cost me a weeks' pay?
Consumed everywhere, unless it's an ice cream on the bay
Synthetic ingredients, quality and profit over simple recipe
Eventually over budget on too many delights, I need therapy.

O stale doughnut, how did you come to be?
Unknown of your origin country
It may be worse, you could be fresh
Too tempting, I'd sell my soul to you, submit my flesh.

Losing my keys

I lost my keys, they weren't losing, they just lost.
It wasn't a football match, but losing came at a cost.
Six hundred of the king's own was a lot.
I'll get a keyring next time.

Friday night, I came home
Saturday I had a day on my own.
Woke up to see both keys had gone awol,
Both of them? How? I couldn't tell you, on my soul!

We searched the house, the rack where they tend to be
The keys grew legs, they must have walked free
Searching through the laundry basket, in the pockets?
Nope! In the legs, do better!
Inside the washing machine? This happened once before.
Nowhere seen, in the sofa? Behind it? Tables and chairs?
Not a bean, nothing, nada, zilch, el zippo.
Could both keys be in the draws? Dotted over our home.
In all the draws, emptied, I found them! I found them!
But not the ones I wanted.

Let's look upstairs? Downstairs? Under the stairs?
Downstairs toilet?
Heating cupboard?

In my shoes, on the bookshelf, in the fridge?
"Stop, Jack! You'll stress yourself out!"

You can't reason with a man on a mission
You can't reason when a man's stressed.
The house was turned upside-down, no keys
Forever a frown, painted a picture of a ton on my face
Both keys gone, stolen? Who's the disgrace?

Come a month, we ordered keys from the dealership.
All programmed, beeped, secured for the car.
Everything was at relief and I felt on cloud nine,
A smell? A banana on the backseat exposed to sunshine
That was my lunch a while ago, never consumed.
My rage re-fulled, I glared into the void of the footwell

Two keys stare at me in a preserved state.
But the new two are in my hand...

...

Fate.

Trip to the Barbershop

What are we having?
Skin fade on the side.

Time flew, not a word spoken;
The mirror display at the end, barber takes pride.

I surrender a purple note of the king.
Most of my hair gone in 30 minutes, I look stunning.

More Martinis

I don't like to drink all the time.
I just like having a good night!
HAAAAA! I scream palely across a room, to no listeners.
I'll have a run outside, I'm bursting with energy!
More alcohol for all! Let's have a great night!
Listened to those who fear for my wellbeing.
My safety could come to danger, I lie on the floor.
I wail of the walls closing in on me, is this a nightmare?
I then got taken to bed, is this a real life mute function?
I didn't have a good time, I inconvenienced everyone else.

No more martinis then.

I Smell Petrol

Smelling strong petrol across the concrete forecourt
Brings back the memories of my youth
I wasn't a ne'er-do-well, just curious, never malicious
The combustible fluid reminded of times in garages
As an adult on my own or as a child with my parents
Parts everywhere, coil springs there, leaking oil from a chair.

Smelling strong diesel coughed up by the family lorry
Even the muscle cars and strong SUVs make way
We never transported crops, nor for shops, just props
Building houses was the family trade that I must follow
Playing with blocks younger, drawing plans older
Sand in the yard, bricks hard, eyeing cement keeping guard.

Smelling strong jet fuel bellows the chamber on G-TAWN
I went to Tenerife on that aged 17, don't ask how I recall
Not an aviation obsessive, in fact my memory's impressive
It rained for just the one day out of seven, for 20 minutes
Teen me flew with my grandparents, present me flew alone
Passport in hand, excursions planned, so many flights to land.

Smelling strong paint boiling off the walls of a fixer-upper
Creaking of the stairs, getting splinters the work is crucial
Rubbish with my hands, can't work the tools, we're fools
Owner in a rut and tempted to burn for insurance purposes
Combustible lead paints, many swatches around, beige, teal
Colour on walls, dust in the halls, broken woodwork tools.

Smelling strong coffee wafting from the machines in a café
Bellowing noises, the cacophony and chatter of the masses
Everyone buys lattés, food on trays, smelling bergamot spray
School books on tables by the young, laptops by the old
Cold drinks for the stylish, hot for the practical
Sandwiches on standby, free Wi-Fi, a local area gentrify.

Smelling strong natural gas emitted by the home boiler
Pipes underground by the... Wait.
I don't have gas in my house.
Purely electric supply, I'm getting high,
Someone sparks something up it'll blow,
Trap that gas and keep the closed window? I die.

7:10 Dreamer

7:10 sunset overdue, this small place
No future here, foreign field, keeps me in town
Wanting more time, people mind their own
Aspirational dreaming, make me a king, wear my crown.

No more lollygagging, I want to work hard
Fill up my time, new motivational lifestyle
The older I get, the less I want to have
All tasks met on time, no more papers to file.

Mission complete, happy life
Now I don't know what to do
I've dreamed it all, the stars are in my reach
Everything I want, need, ask; who else wants this? Who?

Midnighter

Tremble in my bones, look outside tonight
Hair follicles stand to attention.
Taps drip in barren bathroom, towels upon rack
Humming transmitted, random noises scare me sour.

I want to be at peace
I want to be in a dream state
I want to lie flat on sponge surface
I want to close my eyes in splendid silence.

Clocks tick steady rates, times change, many earlies and lates,
Hands switch and swivel, reason and sense turn to drivel
Sanity at stake, all my happiness and serenity you take
Scare me senseless, into submission, shake me cold.

High Street Town Centre

Vape shop, barber shop, betting shop, coffee shop
Vape shop, barber shop, coffee shop, betting shop
Vape shop, coffee shop, betting shop, barber shop
Barber shop, betting shop, coffee shop, vape shop

Bakery, café, book shop, optician
Bakery, café, optician, book shop
Book shop, bakery, optician, café
Café, optician, book shop, bakery

Phone shop, phone shop, phone shop, phone shop
Big brand, Big brand, Independent, Big brand
Big brand, Independent, Big brand, Big brand
Big brand, Big brand, Big brand, Independent

Card shop, jeweller, newly opened barber shop
Card shop, newly opened barber shop, jeweller
Jeweller, card shop, newly opened barber shop
Newly opened barber shop, jeweller, card shop

Shoe shop, bank, here comes another vape shop
Here comes another vape shop, shoe shop, bank
Bank, here comes another vape shop, shoe shop
Shoe shop, here comes another vape shop, bank

Coffee shop, coffee shop, coffee shop, pub
Big chain, big chain, independent, big chain
Independent, big chain, big chain, big chain
Big chain, big chain, big chain, Independent

The footfall in this shopping place is non-transcendent
High streets and town centres anything but resplendent
Hike up business rates, enhanced support and dependence
The family businesses come meek and seek their vengeance.

All the Prime Ministers

1721 is the year for me
Tis the start of Prime Ministers for thee
Many officials and heads of politics
Many facts I can give just for your kicks!

Robert Walpole, he's number 1; 20 years to get jobs done
Spencer Compton, great speaker; to his predecessor merely meeker
Henry Pelham, a peerage he'd shirk, the first PM to die at work
Duke of Newcastle, took over from his bro, lost Menorca, so he's got to go!
Willie Cavendish, appointed with ease, secured cash and men to the colonies
John Stuart, Earl of Bute, the first tory, tall, handsome, astute
George Grenville, raising money yet; he's struggling with French war debt
Marquess Rockingham's resignation, dominated by the American question
Here be PM number nine, Pitt the Elder, he's doing more than fine!
Fitzroy's here, he's rather dim, one of few dukes, he resigned him.
Lord North, apologies; he's lost those precious colonies.
Billy Petty, he's a man of peace; that war with America will finally cease.
Cavendish-Bentinck, rich, had the bling, currently related to our dear King.
Pitt is back, but the son's in power, stop that Napoleon and make him cower!
Addington, the war he couldn't fix, he lived to the ripe age of 86.
Grenville, peace with France wasn't made at least he stopped the slave trade.
Spencer Perceval by a man he was hated, the only PM to be assassinated!
Bobby Jenkinson, a man with clout, he saw Napoleon on his way out!
George Canning, 5 foot 9, a short man and a brief government time;
Freddy Robinson, had 2 sons, stressed in power, but left and he was fine.
Arthur Wellesley, that's Duke of Wellington to you!
Charles Grey, who the tea is named, he was the Earl Grey number two.
Henry Lamb, boring reign, his legacy forgotten as he was mostly at peace;
Bobby Peel, repealed the Corn Laws and made the Met Police.
Known for his bad handling of the Irish Famine, enter Lord Russell,
Eddie Smith-Stanley, the only PM not to have a majority.

George Hamilton-Gordon, to Crimea! Show the world Brits have muscle.
Henry Temple, Viscount Palmerston; the last chap to die on the job.
Benjamin Disraeli, to madame Victoria; he was a god!
William Gladstone, God's only man, one of the greatest of our time.
Robert Cecil, oversaw the Empire expand in record time!
Angering the European elites, Archie Primrose was quickly dispatched.
Arthur Balfour, and his declaration twas a plan he hastily hatched.
Campell-Bannerman what a man, free school meals and workers' rights
Mr. Asquith, to the Somme! World War One, let's have some fights.
David Lloyd George, the sole Welshman in charge of the land,
Bonar-Law, mostly forgotten, one of 2 leaders born on foreign land,
Mr. Baldwin, image tarnished after World War 2,
Ramsay MacDonald, how many parties was he a member? Oh. Two.
Neville Chamberlain, tried to appease with moustache man in Munich.
Enter Churchill, wartime leader, dispatched Mr. Hitler quick!
Clement Attlee, one of the most known and best, founder of our lovely NHS
Eden, Suez disaster, MacMillan ended Profumo affair, truly a mess!
Douglas-Home, he was a Lord you know!
Mr. Wilson smoked a pipe, did he take us to Vietnam? Oh no!
Eddie Heath, to Europe he had a like, Jimmy Callaghan, here's a strike.
Maggie Thatcher, milk snatcher, we got Falklands and we'll keep them thanks!
John Major, Maastricht treaty, Black Wednesday our economy tanks!
Tony Blair, we'll go to Iraq and we'll help our American friends,
Gordon Brown, global recession, the pain never ends,
David Cameron, didn't spend a penny, his government wasn't ready for...
Brexit! Theresa May, tried to sort the mess but couldn't quite be the best,
Boris Johnson our American, had a party during a global endurance test.
Liz Truss, not much to say, economy crashed, only lasted 49 days.
Rishi Sunak, cost of living crisis he couldn't solve, 2024 parliament dissolve;
New man in red, Sir Keir Starmer will he resolve?

Here's my poem to remember the prime ministers of this British land,
It's probably not memorable, great, or noteworthy; it should be banned.

Haiku for the bored

Struggling to engage
I demand such novelties
Can I go home now?

Podcasts

The famous footballer and wife natter on the mic
Relatable, Relatable
Some washed up journalist conversing politics
Debateable, Debateable

Lower those earphones, drum in them earbuds
Indulge in witty banter, they laugh they joke
What's your political standpoint? Right, left, centre?
Involve in the fierce topic, disagree with me? You're woke

This entertainment is a breath a newly-found air to me
It's free, It's free
Find a topic on anything you please, such a wide scope
Let me see, Let me see

Tune in to the sounds, the chatter, the funny lads
Hear their weak arguments, they persuade, they try
Who's this washed up celebrity doing a sponsorship? Who?
Get bored of this podcast, choose another or leave. Goodbye.

Kebabs in the shop

The meat spit on heat, it slowly turns,
Many mouths water, a taste we yearn,
At the end of a long day, or good end to the night,
I'd like it with pitta, and it'll be good food to bite.

Give me the kebab with sauce, give me the chips of course!
Drown it in vinegar, flourised with salt, a dish I endorse.
I'll consume it on the way home from the pub,
Anything so no-one gets their hands on my grub.

I'm gone from the shop, it's late in the night.
Watch on my wrist, tells me it's 2am, a fright!
I can't sleep so I'll go for a stroll;
Neon lights still bright, "mixed grill charcoal".

War is a Lie

In times of war, the rules go deaf.
We'll punish ideological thinkers, we'll put them to death.
It'll be grand, let's shout propaganda to the masses.
Convince the populace, they ain't friends they're foes.
The soldier forced to fight, nothing else going for them,
They won't commit treason at all, their the national stem.
A stem to a flailing tree, ready to fall in the midst of a war.
In the afters of a deal, we'll vilify the weak ones, not forgive.
Conscripts, couldn't pursue paths nor could they choose;
Because in the end, tis only a war crime if you lose.

Haiku for Selling a Car

Solid car for sale,
High mileage on the meter.
One careful owner.

Sunburn Sadness

Beautiful sunshine shimmers from a morning cool,
Heat rapidly rises from the 93 million mile away fireball,
I'm in the pool, surrounded by inflatable floatation aids,
Forgot the re-apply the cream on my shoulders. It's ok I be fine.

Give it hours later, the realisation of one of my many blunders,
My skin red-hot, the temperatures glowing from my shoulders,
Smoulders of dead skin, I need more of that cooling lotion,
Fresh from the fridge, cold showers, shivering, all to no avail.

Can't move, can't think, My mind is occupied by the burn,
Can I raise my arm without being in pain? It hurts when I turn,
Burnt like a fern, I need some fresh, moist, Aloe on the skin,
Dehydrated, cooked to perfection, I now need to try and sleep.

I've been awake for days, the painkillers and creams are a help,
For the previous 48 hours, my pain conveyed by many a yelp,
Welp. The holiday's over and last few days occupied by pain,
Now I'm home back to normalcy, my skin's peeling. Fantastic.

No^No (The Power of No)

"No." is a full sentence,
It be a powerful stand, a weapon of wording.

"No." is a symbol of courage,
Showing your position where it's you versus the globe.

"No." is a mark of independence,
Making your intentions loud and clear.

"No." is a statement of stability,
It shows your reluctance to make a troubling change.

Am I firm on my position? Yes.

Amnesia

Do you suffer from long term memory loss?
I don't think so.

Do you suffer from short term memory loss?
I don't think I do.

Can you please repeat word for word what I just said?
I can't remember.

Neither can I.

What's a Religion?

What's a religion without a god?
Mindless direction, a mere day to give thanks and a nod;
Who do we pray to? To whom do we request mercy?
A wanderer passes, claims they spoke to he/she/it "it's me".

What's a religion without a place of worship?
To what shape shall we build? House? Boat? Turnip?
Who shall garnish our walls? Our creator, or the messenger?
A weekly sermon, our community, for I am a passenger.

What's a religion without a holy script?
The coded rules for our existence and final call on conflict.
Discover the tales and moral stories of all dilemmata.
Always one hero of a fable, make them a saint or martyr.

What's a religion without a following?
Our community strives on one quality, being welcoming.

Haiku for the Painstricken

Get me some tablets
Lower back in agony
Ouch, I need to rest.

Inspirational Messages

March to your own beat.
Old ceilings make new floors.
Who cares? Be content.
SΔnity is pʁiceless.

Taken from the "Inspirational Message" collection of artworks from "Jack Soley's Art Book", published in 2023, ISBN: 9781917706056

Monologue on Wood

What is this meant to be? Art? Poetry? I do not know, these are only words upon wood to me, the creator.

I want my work to gain interest and entice intrigue to you, the reader, the admirer, the curious.

Do the things you've always wanted to try for our time is valuable yet finite, your recent breath or blink could be your last. Do not chase those who won't chase you back.

Take a calculated risk, be brave but not foolish. Laugh, dance, shake hands, respect those close to you. Take care and look after the environment, the world does not revolve around you.

I used to believe the world was perfect, I found out I was wrong a long time ago. This artwork is just words and meaningless sentences with illogical settings.

Listen to the voices that are inside your head when you're in a good state as they are almost always right. A reason for doubt is to prevent stupidity, for it is wise to be cautious.

A life of suspicion will be long lasting, and if you fuck up, so what? Who cares? You did what you did for a valid reason. Look to positive and meaningful people for validation in your life affairs.

Did you see that mistake? You may have spotted the other one closer to the top, I don't like the term 'mistake'; I prefer the word 'challenge' as challenges can be overcome and conquered rather than being left to be problems.

Be independent. Be your master. Seize control and do what gives your existence purpose as nothing is worse than eternal regret.

I shall ask once more, what is this meant to be?

Taken from the "Monologue on Wood" artwork from "Jack Soley's Art Book", published in 2023, ISBN: 9781917706056

Metric World

Let's metricise the world! 1000 grams in a kilo, oh.
Everything's by ten, that's just grand, but also;
By hundreds and thousands, you must be sad?
No, let's preserve the sanity that keeps you from being mad!

Where does it end my lord? 10 days in a week?
Monday to Sunday, with a few oddities in the centre.
Let's make hours 100 minutes with 10 hours a day.
10 months a year, decades be the same, now that's lame.

4.3 weeks in a month average? Make it 5, more sense.
Cash for the most has the right idea, 1 dollar, 100 cents.
What in the world is a pint? I'm not comfortable with 568.
Millilitres? Centilitres? Where am I? What system?

Miles aren't that accurate, kilometres do this ten-ness again.
Luckily we live in a mostly metric world.
It doesn't go overboard, excessive, or berserk;
Confined to the 3 countries, they use it to oath.

Except from Britain, who say they're metric
In reality, we're liars who use both.

Questions That I Can't Find Answers To

I've many questions to answers I can't find.
These thoughts cross my mind, reasons I deny.
I don't find answers as people call me crazy.
Why do we always hire skips but never buy them?

I elevate my enquiries in seriousness, it matters.
I'm rebuffed and ridiculed, my request in tatters.
In my pursuit of knowledge, I'm not allowed to know,
Why do we park on a drive?

Will someone please fulfil my gap of understanding?
I will reward you with peace and no need for knowing.
Mushrooms are truffles, chocolates are too.
But why is one a delight and one a cause of nausea?

Can we ever truly recover a waste of time?
If you've read this prose, probably not.
My apologies.

Tesco Generation

We form part of the neo-cultural Tesco Generation,
Weekly shop with loyalty cards, always buy now, pay later.
We all listen to the same songs on Heart across the nation;
Not a fan of Oasis? Rally against that English traitor.

Off to the football where it's ninety of abusing the referee.
Mindless chatter to the retail staff, what odd things to say.
The age old "if it doesn't scan, that means it's free!".
You're shopping during the 6 hours on Sunday, wasted day.

It's our doctrine to nick the glass after visiting the pub.
Everyone reads the papers for our opinions, Daily Mail.
Eating the monotony on our beige plates, same grub.
Spicy opinions on immigration, put trivial criminals in jail.

We'll do anything to get friends, so we belong in the crowd.
We like who we like, hate who we hate, but forever proud.

Hard to Understand

Sometimes in life;
Norms, customs, rules, and regulations
Aren't always black and white.

Are things clear cut? Or are new traditions
really set in stone?

Can you understand me?
Can you hear me?
Can you feel me?

I am misunderstood.
Or is this just a misunderstanding?

Proverbs To End

99% failure trumps 1% effort,

A past insignificance predicts a future importance.

You can't fall through the floor so you may as well jump.

You've nothing to lose when you're at your lowest.

Habits begin whenever, traditions last forever.

Outroduction

It's been an impressive 3 years, 6 months, and 15 days since I ventured into the unknown universe of writing; this was the moment I became an author. Did I ever envision myself as a poet? Not at all; I began crafting these poems as early as 2018, and many are even more recent. Since last year, I am a man who has no time for regret, and I've finally embraced that radical wake-up call.

Just to be super clear, I'm not a poet, and this is my first dive into the whole poetry thing. I've got a bunch of questions swirling around about this book: How many poems should I include? What topics should I write about? Should I keep it light and fun, or should I try to inject some deeper meaning?

Because this represents my very first venture into the realms of writing poetry, prose, and proverbs that truly express my innermost thoughts, I genuinely felt while crafting these words that I couldn't care less how well it would perform or resonate with others;

as I said in the beginning, it probably won't be a number one bestseller like Clock Worm.

I've reached the conclusion that I cannot afford regrets, and I anticipate that I may take a solid 4-5 years before I consider embarking on another project of this nature again, especially if this book is even remotely regarded as noteworthy or memorable. The pieces within this collection are those thoughts that have floated around in my mind, which I've made it a point to potentially expand on poetry at a later date. I express my gratitude to you for joining me on this journey, and I sincerely hope you find enjoyment in my unique style of storytelling and poetry, and if my work doesn't resonate with you, feel free to critique me; ideally in a public forum online, so that others can join in on the discussion.

And also to harvest free advertising for the book.

Just for fun before I finish for real, do you want to know some rejected titles for this book? Here are some of the best/worst ones:

- Dock Society
- Jack Soley's Poetry Book
- Still Alive Poets Society
- Egg Carpet
- Goodbye Depression, Hello Expression
- Four score and 17 short
- Prose from a Prize Pillock
- Pommy's Poems
- Yes Sir, I Can English.
- It Started At Night Mail
- 99 Wasted Kilobytes
- Oracle of Radical Vision
- Young, Dumb, and Full of Humdrum
- Bruce Springsteen's Box of Custard Creams
- Colonel Mustard's Cupboard of Custard
- Monkey Man's Head Full of Bananas
- Back By Unpopular Demand
- Wannabe Wordsworth from Wiltshire
- Lemchi's Whimsical Compendium of Questionable Wisdom
- With Added Punctuation!
- Mindfullpoetness
- Goodbye Depression and Your Mother Concurs
- Random Poetry from a Random Millennial

- An Adventurers Idea of Poetry for the 21st Century
- Zoof

Acknowledgements

The acknowledgements of this book are the readers and contributors of Writing Magazine, their monthly magazines are stacked up in my house and if I didn't bother subscribing to the magazine I might not have bothered with this book on poetry, prose, and proverbs. Max Fosh for publishing a book on his friends messages to the humour of thousands globally, my best friend Louise for helping me with the artwork that spawned a mildly controversial book published in 2023, and the educators Tom Scott & Michael "Vsauce" Stevens for introducing me to the world of poetic devices.